TWELFTH NIGHT

Shakespeare: The Animated Tales is a multinational venture conceived by S4C, Channel 4 Wales. Produced in Russia, Wales, and England, the series has been financed by S4C, the BBC, and HIT Communications (UK), Christmas Films and Soyuzmultfilm (Russia), Home Box Office (USA), and Fujisankei (Japan).

Academic Panel
Professor Stanley Wells
Dr. Rex Gibson

Academic Co-ordinator
Roy Kendall

Educational Adviser
Michael Marland

Publishing Editor and Co-ordinator
Jane Fior

Book Design
Fiona Macmillan

Animation Director for *Twelfth Night*
Maria Muat of Soyuzmultfilm Studios, Moscow

Series Producer and Director
Dave Edwards of The Dave Edwards Studio Ltd, Cardiff, Wales

Executive Producers
Christopher Grace
Elizabeth Babakhina

Library of Congress Cataloging-in-Publication Data
Garfield, Leon.
    Twelfth night / abridged by Leon Garfield ; illustrated by Ksenia Prytkova.
        p.   cm. — (Shakespeare, the animated tales)
    Summary: An illustrated, abridged version of the Shakespeare comedy with background information and explanatory stage directions.
        ISBN 0–679–83872–4 (pbk.) — ISBN 0–679–93872–9 (lib. bdg.)
    1. Children's plays, English. [1. Plays.] I. Prytkova, Ksenia, ill.
II. Shakespeare, William, 1564–1616. Twelfth night.
III. Title. IV. Series: Garfield, Leon. Shakespeare, the animated tales.
PR2837.A25   1993
822.3'3—dc20   92–14524

Shakespeare

TWELFTH NIGHT

ABRIDGED BY LEON GARFIELD

ILLUSTRATED BY KSENIA PRYTKOVA

ALFRED A. KNOPF · NEW YORK

THE THEATRE IN SHAKESPEARE'S DAY

IN 1989 AN ARCHAEOLOGICAL discovery was made on the south bank of the Thames that sent shivers of delight through the theatre world. A fragment of Shakespeare's own theatre, the Globe, where many of his plays were first performed, had been found.

This discovery has fuelled further interest in how Shakespeare himself conceived and staged his plays. We know a good deal already, and archaeology as well as documentary research will no doubt reveal more, but although we can only speculate on some of the details, we have a good idea of what the Elizabethan theatre-goer saw, heard and smelt when he went to see a play by William Shakespeare at the Globe.

It was an entirely different experience from anything we know today. Modern theatres have roofs to keep out the weather. If it rained on the Globe, forty per cent of the play-goers got wet. The floor of the theatre was packed with a crowd of apprentices, house servants and artisans, who had each paid a penny to stand for the entire duration of the performance.

In the galleries that rose in curved tiers around the inside of the building, sat those who could afford to pay two pennies for a seat and the benefits of a roof over their heads. Here, the middle ranking citizens, the merchants, the sea captains, the clerks from the Inns of Court, would sit crammed into their small eighteen-inch space and look down upon the 'groundlings' below. In the 'Lords room', the rich and the great, noblemen and women, courtiers and foreign ambassadors had to pay sixpence each for the relative comfort and luxury of their exclusive position directly above the stage, where they smoked tobacco, and overlooked the rest.

No dimming lights announced the start of the play. A blast from a trumpet and three sharp knocks warned the audience that the action was about to begin. In the broad daylight, the actor could see the audience as clearly as the audience could see him. He spoke directly to the crowd, and held them with his eyes, following their reactions. He could play up to the raucous laughter that greeted the comical, bawdy scenes, and gauge the emotional response to the higher flights of poetry. Sometimes he even improvised speeches of his own. He was surrounded by, enfolded by his audience. And it was the words that moved them. They came to listen, rather than to see.

In 1613 the Globe theatre was set on fire by a spark from a cannon during a performance of Henry VIII, and it burnt to the ground. The actors, including Shakespeare himself, dug into their own pockets and paid for it to be rebuilt. The new theatre lasted until 1642, when it closed again. Now, in the 1990s, the Globe is set to rise again as a committed band of actors, scholars and enthusiasts are raising the money to rebuild Shakespeare's theatre in its original form a few yards from its previous site.

From the time when the first Globe theatre was built until today, Shakespeare's plays have been performed in a vast variety of languages, styles, costumes and techniques, on stage, on film, on television and in animated film. Shakespeare himself, working within the round wooden walls of his theatre, would have been astonished by it all.

Patrick Spottiswoode
Director Globe Education,
Shakespeare Globe Trust

WILLIAM SHAKESPEARE

NEXT TO GOD, A wise man once said, Shakespeare created most. In the thirty-seven plays that are his chief legacy to the world—and surely no-one ever left a richer legacy!—human nature is displayed in all its astonishing variety.

He has enriched the stage with matchless comedies, tragedies, histories, and, towards the end of his life, with plays that defy all description, strange plays that haunt the imagination like visions.

His range is enormous: kings and queens, priests, princes and merchants, soldiers, clowns and drunkards, murderers, pimps, whores, fairies, monsters and pale, avenging ghosts 'strut and fret their hour upon the stage'. Murders and suicides abound; swords flash, blood flows, poison drips, and lovers sigh; yet there is always time for old men to talk of growing apples and for gardeners to discuss the weather.

His life, from what we know of it, was not astonishing. There are no duels, no loud, passionate loves, no excesses of any kind. He was not one of your unruly geniuses whose habits are more interesting than their works. From all accounts, he was of a gentle, honourable disposition, a good businessman, and a careful father.

He was born on April 23rd 1564, to John and Mary Shakespeare of Henley Street, Stratford-upon-Avon. He was their third child and first son. When he was four or five he began his education at the local petty school. He left the local grammar school when he was about fourteen, in all probability to help in his father's glove-making shop. When he was eighteen, he married Anne Hathaway, who lived in a nearby village. By the time he was twenty-one, he was the father of three children, two daughters and a son.

Then, it seems, a restless mood came upon him. Maybe he travelled, maybe he was, as some say, a schoolmaster in the country; but at some time during the next seven years, he went to London and found employment in the theatre. When he was twenty-eight, he was already well enough known as an actor and playwright to excite the spiteful envy of a rival, who referred to him as 'an upstart crow'.

He mostly lived and worked in London until his mid-forties, when he returned to his family and home in Stratford, where he remained in prosperous circumstances until his death on April 23rd 1616, his fifty-second birthday. He left behind him a widow, two daughters (his son died in childhood), and the richest imaginary world ever created by the human mind.

TWELFTH NIGHT

'What country, my friends, is this?' asks a young woman on a strange seashore; and the answer comes: 'This is Illyria, lady.' And so the story begins.

Illyria: land of a lovesick duke, a countess in deep mourning, her drunken uncle and his rowdy friends, and a solemn steward with a face as long as Sunday, who thinks, because he is virtuous, there should be no more cakes and ale. Then, into this world, comes a pair of shipwrecked twins to wreak havoc among hearts and heads; and through it all, like a vein of dancing quicksilver, run the songs and wit of Feste, the jester, the wisest fool in the land: for he is paid to play the fool, while the rest of Illyria does it for nothing.

Shakespeare wrote the play when he was about thirty-seven, just after the tragic *Hamlet* and just before the bitter *Troilus and Cressida*; though all it has in common with its stern neighbours is the genius of its creator.

The title refers to an ancient Festival of Fools, a time of carnival, when everything is turned upside down, when blindfold love blunders in a circle, forever missing his mark.

Shakespeare gave the play an alternative title: '*What You Will*', as if to offer the audience its own choice. King Charles I liked to call it '*Malvolio*', after his favourite character; but the play is so rich in favourites, that the world has decided not to meddle in choices, and leave it at '*Twelfth Night*'.

LEON GARFIELD

THE CHARACTERS IN THE PLAY
in order of appearance

ORSINO	*Duke of Illyria*
SIR TOBY BELCH	*Olivia's kinsman*
MARIA	*Olivia's waiting-gentlewoman*
SIR ANDREW AGUECHEEK	*Sir Toby's companion*
VIOLA	*later disguised as Cesario*
CAPTAIN	*of the wrecked ship, befriending Viola*
COURTIER	
LUTE PLAYER	
OLIVIA	*a countess*
FESTE	*jester to Olivia*
MALVOLIO	*Olivia's steward*
SEBASTIAN	*Viola's twin brother*
ANTONIO	*a sea-captain, befriending Sebastian*
SERVANT	*of Olivia*
OFFICER	*in the service of the Duke*
PRIEST	

The curtain rises on a wild sea upon which a fragile vessel is being tossed to and fro. Tremendous waves pound its sides as if to smash it like an egg-shell; and tiny figures fling themselves over the sides and strike out desperately for land.

Beyond its wild sea coast, Illyria is a green and pleasant land, ruled over by the Duke Orsino, a gentleman made melancholy by unrequited love . . .

In the Duke's mansion, he sits, listening to the sad music of a lute-player. Presently the music ceases.

DUKE   If music be the food of love, play on, give me excess of it . . .

As the lute-player resumes, the duke rises and goes to a window and gazes out towards a distant mansion. He sighs, for within that mansion is his love. She is the Countess Olivia, and she will have nothing to do with him.

In Olivia's house, all is sober and hung with black, for she is in mourning for a dead brother and has vowed to admit no thoughts of love for seven long years. But though all is mournful above stairs, in the wine cellar, like a stormy stomach below a calm face, riot ferments and bubbles in the person of her boozy uncle, Sir Toby Belch. He is with Maria, the countess's pretty waiting-woman.

SIR TOBY   What a plague means my niece to take the death of her brother thus? I am sure care's an enemy to life.

MARIA   By my troth, Sir Toby, you must come in earlier a'nights. Your cousin, my lady, takes great exception to your ill hours.

SIR TOBY   Why, let her except before excepted. (*He drinks.*)

MARIA   That quaffing and drinking will undo you: I heard my lady talk of it yesterday; and of a foolish knight that you brought in one night to be her wooer.

SIR TOBY   Who, Sir Andrew Aguecheek?

MARIA   Ay, he.

SIR TOBY   He's as tall as any man in Illyria!

MARIA   What's that to th'purpose?

SIR TOBY   Why, he has three thousand ducats a year.

MARIA	He's a very fool and a prodigal. He's drunk nightly in your company!
SIR TOBY	With drinking healths to my niece! I'll drink to her as long as there is a passage in my throat, and drink in Illyria! Here comes Sir Andrew Agueface!

Enter Sir Andrew Aguecheek, a tall, thin, fair-haired gentleman. He bows gallantly to Maria.

SIR ANDREW	Bless you, fair shrew!
MARIA	And you too, sir.
SIR ANDREW	Shall we not set about some revels?
SIR TOBY	What else shall we do? (*Gives Sir Andrew a drink.*) Let me see thee caper! (*Sir Andrew drinks and begins to dance, somewhat wildly.*) Ha, higher, higher!

Sir Toby joins in the dance and the two gentlemen clutch at Maria, who, helpless with laughter, evades them and makes her escape.

The sea-shore. A storm-battered boat lies on the beach and, beside it, some half dozen survivors from the shipwreck: among them is a young woman, Viola.

VIOLA	What country, friends, is this?
CAPTAIN	This is Illyria, lady.
VIOLA	And what should I do in Illyria? My brother, he is in Elysium. (*She gazes sadly out to sea.*) Perchance he is not drowned: what think you, sailors?
CAPTAIN	It is perchance that you yourself were saved.
VIOLA	O my poor brother! and so perchance may he be!
CAPTAIN	True, madam, and to comfort you with chance, assure yourself—After our ship did split, I saw your brother bind himself to a strong mast that lived upon the sea. I saw him hold acquaintance with the waves so long as I could see.
VIOLA	For saying so, there's gold! Knowest thou this country?
CAPTAIN	Ay, madam.
VIOLA	Who governs here?
CAPTAIN	Orsino.
VIOLA	Orsino! I have heard my father name him. I'll serve this duke. Thou shalt present me as an eunuch to him . . .

The captain nods, and Viola clasps him gratefully by the hand.

So Viola, with the captain's help, becomes Cesario, a page, and attired as a man, serves the duke in his palace.

COURTIER　If the duke continues these favours towards you, Cesario, you are like to be much advanced; he hath known you but three days and already you are no stranger.

The duke enters. Viola gazes at him, and it is evident that her feelings towards him are somewhat stronger than those of a page for his master.

DUKE　Cesario, thou knowest no less but all: I have unclasped to thee the book even of my secret soul. (*He goes to the window and gazes towards the mansion of Olivia.*) Therefore, good youth, address thy gait unto her, be not denied access, stand at her doors, and tell them, there thy fixed foot shall grow till thou have audience.

VIOLA　Say I do speak with her, my lord, what then?

DUKE　O then unfold the passion of my love.

VIOLA　I'll do my best to woo your lady. (*She takes her departure, glancing back at the lovesick duke.*) Yet . . . whoe'er I woo, myself would be his wife!

As Viola departs, the duke signs to his lute-player, who sings:

LUTE-PLAYER
　　　　　Come away, come away death,
　　　　　And in sad cypress let me be laid.
　　　　　Fly away, fly away breath,
　　　　　I am slain by a fair cruel maid . . .

The fair cruel maid is Olivia in her mansion, all in black. She is attended by solemn servants, and Feste, her jester, who tries, vainly, to make her smile.

OLIVIA   Take the fool away.

FESTE   Do you not hear, fellows? Take away the lady.

OLIVIA   Sir, I bade them take away you.

FESTE   Misprision in the highest degree! Good madonna, give me leave to prove you a fool.

OLIVIA   Can you do it?

FESTE   Dexteriously, madam. Good madonna, why mourn'st thou?

OLIVIA   Good fool, for my brother's death.

FESTE   I think his soul is in hell, madonna.

OLIVIA   I know his soul is in heaven, fool.

FESTE   The more fool, madonna, to mourn for your brother's soul, being in heaven. Take away the fool, gentlemen!

Maria enters with Olivia's steward, Malvolio, a solemn, long-faced personage, who looks exceedingly disapprovingly at the jester.

MARIA   Madam, there is at the gate a young gentleman much desires to speak with you.

OLIVIA   Tell him he shall not speak with me.

MALVOLIO   He has been told so; and says he'll stand at your door like a sheriff's post . . .

OLIVIA   What manner of man?

MALVOLIO   Of very ill manner: he'll speak with you, will you or no.

OLIVIA   Of what personage and years is he?

MALVOLIO   Not yet old enough for a man, nor young enough for a boy; as a squash is before 'tis a peascod. 'Tis with him in standing water, between boy and man.

OLIVIA   (*wearily*) Let him approach. (*Malvolio departs. Olivia turns to her maid, Maria.*) Give me my veil: come, throw it o'er my face. We'll once more hear Orsino's embassy.

Maria veils her mistress's face, and, with other black-gowned ladies of Olivia's court, stands behind her. Viola enters with a gallant flourish of her plumed cap. She is every inch the gentleman, and, one might say, with inches over and to spare.

VIOLA   The honourable lady of the house, which is she?

OLIVIA   Speak to me. I shall answer for her.

VIOLA   Most radiant, exquisite and unmatchable beauty—I pray you, tell me if this be the lady of the house, for I never saw her. I would be loath to cast away my speech. Are you the lady of the house?

OLIVIA   I am. Speak your office.

VIOLA   It alone concerns your ear.

Olivia gazes at the 'young man' thoughtfully.

OLIVIA   Give us this place alone. (*The attendants depart.*) Now sir, what is your text?

VIOLA   In Orsino's bosom.

OLIVIA   O, I have read it: it is heresy. Have you no more to say?

Viola stares curiously at the veiled face before her.

VIOLA   Good madam, let me see your face.

OLIVIA   Have you any commission from your lord to negotiate with my face? You are now out of your text; but we will draw the curtain, and show you the picture. (*She draws aside her veil.*) Is't not well done?

VIOLA   Excellently done, if God did all.

OLIVIA   'Tis in grain, sir, 'twill endure wind and weather.

VIOLA   'Tis beauty truly blent. Lady, you are the cruell'st she alive if you would lead these graces to the grave and leave the world no copy. My lord and master loves you. If I did love you in my master's flame, in your denial I would find no sense; I would not understand it.

OLIVIA   Why, what would you?

VIOLA   Make me a willow cabin at your gate, and call upon my soul within the house; write loyal cantons of contemnèd love, and sing them loud even in the dead of night; halloo your name to the reverberate hills, and make the babbling gossip of the air cry out 'Olivia!' O, you should not rest between the elements of earth and air but you should pity me!

OLIVIA   You might do much. What is your parentage?

VIOLA   Above my fortunes.

OLIVIA   Get you to your lord: I cannot love him: let him send no more, unless, perchance, you come to me again . . .

VIOLA   (*bowing her way out*) Farewell, fair cruelty!

Olivia gazes after the departed 'young man'. She sighs, and her eyes are filled with a sudden tenderness.

OLIVIA   What is your parentage? Above my fortunes. (*She sighs again.*) Malvolio!

The gloomy steward enters. Olivia beckons him close and murmurs to him.

Viola, her embassy completed as unsuccessfully as she could have wished, strides along the road towards the duke's palace. But she is being followed. Malvolio, his black coat flapping and his skinny black legs twinkling, hastens to overtake her.

MALVOLIO   Were you not even now with the Countess Olivia?

VIOLA   Even now, sir.

MALVOLIO   She returns this ring to you, sir. (*Disdainfully he holds out a ring to her. Viola stares at it, bewildered. Malvolio shrugs his shoulders, and drops it on the ground.*) If it be worth stooping for, there it lies: if not, be it his that finds it. (*He stalks away. Viola picks up the ring.*)

VIOLA   I left no ring with her: what means this lady? (*She is suddenly alarmed.*) She loves me, sure! Poor lady, she were better love a dream!

In the wine-cellar of the Countess's house, Feste, her fool, is singing to Sir Toby and Sir Andrew, while round about, like music-charmed monsters, great barrels and bottles wink and sway in the candlelight.

FESTE
O mistress mine, where are you roaming?
O stay and hear, your true love's coming,
That can sing both high and low.
Trip no further, pretty sweeting;
Journeys end in lovers meeting,
Every wise man's son doth know . . .

SIR ANDREW   A mellifluous voice, as I am a true knight.

SIR TOBY   But shall we make the welkin dance indeed?

SIR ANDREW   Let's do it! Come, begin!

They begin to sing a round, with much banging of tankards on the table. Maria enters, in her night attire.

MARIA   What a caterwauling do you keep here! (*Sir Toby catches her round the waist and, despite her protests, whirls her off in a drunken dance. The uproar continues. Malvolio enters, grim as death at a wedding.*)

MALVOLIO   My masters, are you mad? Have you no wit, manners nor honesty but to gabble like tinkers at this time of night?

The dance comes to a panting conclusion.

SIR TOBY   Dost thou think because thou art virtuous there shall be no more cakes and ale?

MALVOLIO   (*grimly*) She shall know of it. (*He points meaningly upward, and stalks away.*)

MARIA   Go shake your ears. (*She shakes her fist after the pompous steward.*) For Monsieur Malvolio, let me alone with him! If I do not gull him, do not think I have wit enough to lie straight in my bed: I know I can do it!

SIR TOBY   What wilt thou do?

MARIA   I will drop in his way some obscure epistles of love. I can write very like my lady, your niece—

SIR TOBY   Excellent, I smell a device!

SIR ANDREW   I have it in my nose too!

SIR TOBY   He shall think by the letters that thou wilt drop that they come from my niece, and that she's in love with him.

MARIA   My purpose is indeed a horse of that colour.

Maria departs.

SIR TOBY   Let's to bed, knight. Thou hadst need send for more money.

SIR ANDREW   If I cannot recover your niece, I am a foul way out.

SIR TOBY   Send for money, knight; if thou hast her not i' the end, call me cut.

In Orsino's palace, the duke has received the unhappy news of the failure of his embassy. Viola stands in attendance.

DUKE   Once more, Cesario, get thee to yon same sovereign cruelty. Tell her my love . . .

VIOLA   But if she cannot love you?

DUKE   I cannot be so answered.

VIOLA   Sooth, but you must. Say that some lady, as perhaps there is, hath for your love as great a pang of heart as you have for Olivia—

DUKE   —Make no compare between that love a woman can bear me, and that I owe Olivia!

VIOLA   Ay, but I know—

DUKE   What dost thou know?

VIOLA   Too well what love women to men may owe. My father had a daughter loved a man as it might be, perhaps, were I a woman, I should your lordship.

DUKE   And what's her history?

VIOLA   A blank, my lord. She never told her love, but let concealment, like a worm i' the bud, feed on her damask cheek; she pined in thought, and with a green and yellow melancholy she sat like Patience on a monument, smiling at grief. Was not this love indeed?

DUKE   But died thy sister of her love, my boy?

VIOLA   I am all the daughters of my father's house, and all the brothers, too—and yet I know not. Sir, shall I to this lady?

Orsino nods.

The garden of Olivia's mansion. It is a maze of intersecting paths and high box hedges. Like witty insects of the larger sort, Sir Toby, Sir Andrew and Maria scurry hither and thither and, finding a suitable path, drop a letter upon it. Then they vanish behind the hedges. Presently, solemn as an aged beetle, Malvolio comes strolling along. As he walks, he muses, and reveals to the unseen watchers, his secret self.

MALVOLIO 'Tis but fortune, all is fortune. Maria once told me she did affect me . . . To be Count Malvolio! There's an example for it: the Lady of the Strachy married the yeoman of the wardrobe. Having been three months married to her, sitting in my state— (*He sees the letter. He frowns, then glancing cautiously about him, bends and picks it up. He studies it.*) By my life, this is my lady's hand! 'To the unknown beloved.' To whom should this be? (*He breaks the seal and begins to read.*) 'Jove knows I love, but who? Lips do not move: no man must know. M.O.A.I. doth sway my life.' M.O.A.I. Every one of these letters are in my name! 'If this fall into thy hand, revolve.' (*He revolves.*) 'In my stars I am above thee, but be not afraid of greatness. Some are born great, some achieve greatness, some have greatness thrust upon 'em. Thy fates open their hands. Remember who

commended thy yellow stockings and wished to see thee ever cross-gartered: I say, remember. Go to, thou art made if thou desirest to be so; if not, let me see thee steward still.' This is open! 'Thou canst not choose to know who I am. If thou entertain'st my love, let it appear in thy smiling. Thy smiles become thee well.' Jove, I thank thee! I will smile; I will do everything that thou wilt have me!

Malvolio, overwhelmed by his good fortune, skips and capers away. The conspirators emerge from concealment, shaking with laughter and delight at the success of their plot. Maria and Sir Toby make off; Sir Andrew lingers, for he has seen that Olivia, attended by a lady, approaches. Sir Andrew steps forward and executes a courtly bow. Olivia ignores him, for she has seen Viola approaching.

VIOLA   (*bowing*) Most excellent accomplished lady, the heavens rain odours on you!

Sir Andrew backs away and secretes himself behind a hedge.

SIR ANDREW   That youth's a rare courtier—'rain odours'—well!

Olivia dismisses her companion and sits upon a rustic bench.

OLIVIA   Give me your hand, sir.

VIOLA   My duty, madam, and most humble service. (*Offers a hand. Olivia seizes it and pulls Viola to sit beside her.*) Dear lady—

OLIVIA   Give me leave, beseech you. What is your name?

VIOLA   Cesario is your servant's name, fair princess.

OLIVIA   My servant, sir? Y'are servant to the Count Orsino, youth.

VIOLA   Madam, I come to whet your gentle thoughts on his behalf—

OLIVIA   I bade you never speak of him again—

VIOLA   You'll nothing, madam, to my lord, by me? (*She tries to escape.*)

OLIVIA   Stay! Cesario, by the roses of the spring, by maidenhood, honour, truth and everything, I love thee—

VIOLA   (*at last escaping from Olivia's loving clutches*) Adieu, good madam; never more will I my master's tears to you deplore!

OLIVIA   Yet come again!

She holds out her arms to the fast vanishing Viola.

In the wine-cellar of Olivia's mansion, Sir Toby and Maria are together. They are joined by a bewildered and hurt Sir Andrew.

SIR ANDREW   I saw your niece do more favours to the count's servingman than ever she bestowed on me!

SIR TOBY   Why then, challenge me the count's youth to fight with him, hurt him in eleven places. There is no love-maker in the world can more prevail in man's commendation with women than report of valour!

MARIA   There is no way but this, Sir Andrew.

They look at one another. Sir Andrew draws his sword and flourishes it. He will take the good advice, and challenge the youth to a duel.

In the town, a perfect image of Viola is walking with a gentleman. It is Sebastian, her twin brother, who, like herself, has been saved from the sea.

SEBASTIAN   You must know of me then, Antonio, my name is Sebastian. Some hour before you took me from the breach of the sea was my sister drowned.

ANTONIO   Alas, the day!

SEBASTIAN   What's to do? Shall we go see the relics of this town?

ANTONIO   Would you'd pardon me. I do not without danger walk these streets. Once in a sea-fight 'gainst the Count his galleys, I did some service. If I be lapsed in this place I shall pay dear.

SEBASTIAN   Do not walk then too open.

ANTONIO   It doth not fit me. Hold, sir, here's my purse. In the south suburbs, at the Elephant, is best to lodge. (*He offers his purse to Sebastian.*)

SEBASTIAN   Why I your purse?

ANTONIO   Haply your eye shall light upon some toy you have desire to purchase.

SEBASTIAN   I'll be your purse-bearer and leave you for an hour . . .

They part.

In Olivia's mansion, the lady is seated with Maria.

OLIVIA   Where's Malvolio? He is sad and civil, and suits well for a servant with my fortunes. Where is Malvolio?

MARIA   (*going to the door*) He is coming, madam, but in a very strange manner.

Malvolio enters. He is solemnly black above, but riotously yellow below; and his skinny legs are imprisoned in black-cross-gartering, like starved canaries in a cage. He is smiling with great determination.

OLIVIA   (*amazed*) How now, Malvolio?

MALVOLIO   (*roguishly*) Sweet lady, ho, ho!

OLIVIA   Smil'st thou? I sent for thee upon a sad occasion.

MALVOLIO   Sad, lady? I could be sad. (*He tries to loosen his garters.*) This does make some obstruction in the blood, this cross-gartering. But what of that?

OLIVIA   What is the matter with thee? Wilt thou go to bed, Malvolio?

MALVOLIO   (*reacting with surprise and delight*) To bed? Ay, sweetheart, and I'll come to thee!

OLIVIA   What mean'st thou by that, Malvolio?

MALVOLIO   Some are born great—

OLIVIA   Ha?

MALVOLIO   Some achieve greatness—

OLIVIA   What say'st thou?

MALVOLIO   And some have greatness thrust upon them! (*He attempts to embrace Olivia who reacts with horror.*)

OLIVIA   Heavens restore thee! This is very midsummer madness!

A servant enters.

SERVANT   Madam, the young gentleman of the Count Orsino's is returned—

OLIVIA   I'll come to him. (*To Maria*) Good Maria, let this fellow be looked to. Let some of my people have a special care of him.

Exit Olivia. Sir Toby's inflamed face appears round the door, followed by the portly rest of him.

MALVOLIO   Go hang yourselves all; you are idle, shallow things, I am not of your element.

He stalks away. Sir Toby and Maria look at one another happily.

SIR TOBY   Come, we'll have him in a dark room and bound. My niece is already in the belief he's mad . . .

At the gate of the mansion where Olivia has hastened to meet Viola, and to renew her protestations of love. They have not been well received.

OLIVIA   I have said too much unto a heart of stone.

VIOLA   With the same haviour that your passion bears goes on my master's grief.

OLIVIA   Here, wear this jewel for me, 'tis my picture. Refuse it not, it hath no tongue to vex you. What shall you ask of me that I'll deny?

VIOLA   Nothing but this: your true love for my master.

OLIVIA   How with mine honour may I give him that which I have given to you?

VIOLA   (*departing*) I will acquit you.

OLIVIA   Well, come again tomorrow. Fare thee well.

Olivia retires. Viola begins to walk away, but is accosted by Sir Toby and Feste, the jester.

SIR TOBY   Gentleman, God save thee.

VIOLA   And you, sir.

SIR TOBY   That defence thou hast, betake thee to it. (*He points to Viola's sword.*)

VIOLA   (*uneasily*) You mistake, sir: I am sure no man hath any quarrel with me.

SIR TOBY   You'll find it otherwise, I assure you. Therefore, if you hold your life at any price, betake you to your guard: for your opposite has in him what youth, strength, skill and wrath, can furnish a man withal.

VIOLA	I pray you, sir, what is he?
SIR TOBY	He is a knight. Souls and bodies hath he divorced three.
VIOLA	(*trembling*) I will return again into the house. I am no fighter.
SIR TOBY	Sir, no. (*He bars Viola's way.*)
VIOLA	I beseech you, do me this courteous office, as to know of the knight what my offence to him is.
SIR TOBY	I will do so. (*He turns to Feste*) Stay by this gentleman till my return.

Sir Toby departs. Viola eyes Feste. She tries to make off. Deftly, Feste dances in front of her. There is no escape.

VIOLA	I beseech you, what manner of man is he?
FESTE	He is indeed, sir, the most skilful, bloody and fatal opposite that you could possibly have found in any part of Illyria.

While Feste is preparing Viola for the worst outside the gate, within it, Sir Toby is performing the same office for the petrified Sir Andrew.

SIR TOBY	Why, man, he is a very devil, I have not seen such a firago. They say he has been fencer to the Sophy.
SIR ANDREW	Pox on't, I'll not meddle with him!
SIR TOBY	Ay, but he will not now be pacified.

Sir Andrew tries to make off, but Sir Toby holds him fast. Outside the gate, Feste is likewise holding Viola. The gate is opened and the two combatants are thrust towards one another.

VIOLA	Pray God defend me! A little thing would make me tell them how much I lack of a man!
SIR TOBY	Come, Sir Andrew, there's no remedy.
VIOLA	I do assure you, 'tis against my will!

Viola and Sir Andrew draw swords and, with faces averted, advance towards one another. But before their blades can touch, they are interrupted. Antonio appears. Instantly, he draws his own sword and parts the duellists.

ANTONIO   Put up your sword! If this young gentleman have done offence, I'll take the fault on me!

There is general amazement; but before it can be resolved, officers come upon the scene and instantly seize Antonio.

OFFICER   Antonio, I arrest thee at the suit of Count Orsino!

ANTONIO   I must obey. (*To Viola*) This comes with seeking you. Now my necessity makes me to ask you for my purse.

Viola stares at him blankly.

OFFICER   Come, sir, away.

ANTONIO   I must entreat you for some of that money.

VIOLA   What money, sir?

ANTONIO   Will you deny me now? Is't possible that my deserts to you can lack persuasion?

VIOLA   I know of none, nor know I you by voice or any feature.

ANTONIO	O heavens themselves!
OFFICER	Come sir, I pray you go.
ANTONIO	This youth that you see here I snatched one half out of the jaws of death—
OFFICER	What's that to us? The time goes by. Away!
ANTONIO	O how vile an idol proves this god! Thou hast, Sebastian, done good feature shame.
OFFICER	The man grows mad. Away with him! Come, come, sir. (*Antonio is led away.*)
VIOLA	He named Sebastian! O if it prove, tempests are kind and salt waves fresh in love!

Before Sir Toby can stop her, she runs away.

| SIR TOBY | A very dishonest paltry boy, and more coward than hare. |
| SIR ANDREW | I'll after him again, and beat him! |

They are about to set off when, to their great surprise, their quarry approaches from the opposite direction. It is Sebastian.

| SIR ANDREW | (*fiercely*) Now sir, have I met you again? There's for you! |

He strikes at Sebastian with his sword. Sebastian, astonished and outraged to find himself so unreasonably set upon, returns the blow with interest.

SEBASTIAN   Why there's for thee, and there, and there!

SIR TOBY   Come on, sir, hold! (*He attempts to intervene.*)

SEBASTIAN   What wouldst thou now? Draw thy sword!

Sir Toby draws; however, at the first clash of steel, Olivia appears.

OLIVIA   Hold, Toby! on thy life, I charge thee, hold!

The combatants part.

SIR TOBY   (*contritely*) Madam!

OLIVIA   Ungracious wretch! Out of my sight! (*Sir Toby, Sir Andrew and Feste hastily depart. Olivia turns to Sebastian.*) I prithee, gentle friend, go with me to my house. (*Sebastian stands and gapes. Olivia takes him by the hand and draws him within the gate.*) Thou shalt not choose but go. Do not deny . . .

Sebastian, dazedly, suffers himself to be led by the lovely Olivia.

SEBASTIAN   If it be thus to dream, still let me sleep.

They go into the mansion.
  Even as Sebastian is in a dream of heaven, Malvolio is in a dream of hell. He has been confined, as a madman, in a dark room with a barred door. Feste, in the guise of a priest, one Sir Topaz, visits him, while Sir Toby and Maria listen eagerly to what passes, as Feste and Malvolio converse through the bars.

MALVOLIO   Do not think I am mad! They have laid me here in hideous darkness!

FESTE   Fie, thou dishonest Satan! Say'st thou the house is dark?

MALVOLIO   As hell, Sir Topaz!

FESTE   Madman, thou errest. There is no darkness but ignorance. Fare thee well.

MALVOLIO   Sir Topaz, Sir Topaz!

SIR TOBY   To him, in thine own voice! (*Sir Toby and Maria depart.*)

FESTE   (*in his own voice*) Alas, sir, how fell you beside your five wits?

MALVOLIO   I am as well in my wits, fool, as thou art.

FESTE   But as well? Then you are mad indeed, if you be no better in your wits than a fool!

MALVOLIO   Good fool, help me to some light and some paper. I tell thee I am as well in my wits as any man in Illyria! Some ink, paper and light, and convey what I will set down to my lady!

FESTE   (*sings*)

> I am gone, sir, and anon, sir,
> I'll be with you again . . .

In Olivia's garden, Sebastian muses on his good fortune.

SEBASTIAN   This may be some error, but no madness, yet doth this accident and flood of fortune so far exceed all instance, all discourse, that I am ready to distrust mine eyes, and wrangle with my reason that persuades me to any other trust but that I am mad, or else the lady's mad . . . But here the lady comes!

Olivia approaches, dragging in her wake, a priest, a real one.

OLIVIA   Blame not this haste of mine. If you mean well, now go with me and with this holy man into the chantry by; there before him, plight me the full assurance of your faith. What do you say?

Sebastian stares about him, as if weighing up all the advantages of the match.

SEBASTIAN   I'll follow this good man, and go with you, and having sworn truth, ever will be true.

OLIVIA   Then lead the way, good father.

Vigorously, she propels the priest towards the chapel wherein all her dreams will soon come true.

Outside the gate of the mansion, the duke and Viola, with lords in attendance, approach. Feste, leaning against the gatepost, bows and holds out his hand. The duke drops a coin into it.

DUKE   If you will let your lady know I am here to speak with her, and bring her along with you, it may awaken my bounty further.

Feste departs into the house. A group of officers approach. In their midst is their prisoner, Antonio.

VIOLA   Here comes the man, sir, that did rescue me.

OFFICER   Orsino, this is that Antonio that took the Phoenix—

VIOLA   He did me kindness, sir—

DUKE   Notable pirate, what foolish boldness brought thee—

ANTONIO   A witchcraft drew me hither. That most ungrateful boy there by your side! For his sake did I expose myself into the danger of this adverse town; drew to defend him when he was beset; where, being apprehended, his false cunning denied me mine own purse, which I had recommended to his use not half an hour before!

VIOLA   How can this be?

Olivia, attended, appears at the gate. She sees Viola.

OLIVIA   Cesario, you do not keep promise with me.

VIOLA   Madam—

DUKE   Gracious Olivia—

OLIVIA   (*ignoring the duke*) What do you say, Cesario?

VIOLA   My lord would speak—

OLIVIA   If it be aught to the old tune, my lord, it is as fat and fulsome to
mine ear as howling after music.

DUKE   Still so cruel?

OLIVIA   Still so constant, my lord.

Orsino sighs, and turns to Viola

DUKE   Come, boy, with me. (*The duke turns to leave. Viola does
likewise.*)

OLIVIA   Where goes Cesario?

VIOLA   After him I love.

OLIVIA   Hast thou forgot thyself? Is it so long?

DUKE   Come away.

OLIVIA	Cesario, husband, stay!
DUKE	Husband?
OLIVIA	Ay, husband. Can he deny?
DUKE	(*to Viola*) Her husband, sirrah?
VIOLA	Not I, my lord!

As all look to one another in disgust, anger, and uncomprehending terror, the priest appears.

OLIVIA	O welcome, father! I charge thee, by thy reverence, here to unfold what thou dost know hath newly passed between this youth and me.
PRIEST	A contract of eternal bond of love—

DUKE   O thou dissembling cub! Farewell, and take her—

VIOLA   (*in tears*) My lord, I do protest—

Sir Andrew comes staggering, bleeding from his head.

SIR ANDREW   (*gasping*) For the love of God, a surgeon! Send one presently to Sir Toby!

OLIVIA   Who has done this, Sir Andrew?

SIR ANDREW   The Count's gentleman, one Cesario. 'Od's lifelings, here he is! You broke my head for nothing!

VIOLA   Why do you speak to me? I never hurt you.

Now comes Sir Toby, also bleeding, and assisted by Feste.

DUKE   How now, gentleman, how is't with you?

SIR TOBY   That's all one. H'as hurt me, (*pointing to Viola*) and there's
           th'end on't.

OLIVIA   Get him to bed, and let his hurt be looked to.

*Sir Andrew, Sir Toby and Feste depart. No sooner have they
gone than Sebastian appears.*

SEBASTIAN   I am sorry, madam, I have hurt your kinsman: But had it been the brother of my blood, I must have done no less with wit and safety. You throw a strange regard upon me, and by that I do perceive it hath offended you. Pardon me, sweet one, even for the vows we made each other but so late ago.

All are suddenly dumb with amazement, as they look from Sebastian to Viola.

DUKE   One face, one voice, one habit, and two persons! A natural perspective, that is, and is not!

SEBASTIAN   (*seeing Antonio*) Antonio, O my dear Antonio! How have the hours racked and tortured me, since I have lost thee!

ANTONIO	Sebastian are you?
OLIVIA	Most wonderful!

Sebastian and Viola now see one another.

SEBASTIAN	Do I stand there? I never had a brother. What kin are you to me?
VIOLA	Sebastian was my father; such a Sebastian was my brother too: so went he suited to his watery tomb. If spirits can assume both form and suit, you come to fright us.
SEBASTIAN	Thrice welcome, drowned Viola! (*To Olivia*) So comes it, lady, you have been mistook. You would have been contracted to a maid; nor are you therein, by my life, deceived: you are betrothed both to a maid and man.

Olivia stares uncertainly at her husband.

DUKE   Be not amazed, right noble is his blood. (*Olivia and Sebastian join hands.*) If this be so, as yet the glass seems true, I shall have share in this most happy wreck. (*To Viola*) Boy, thou hast said to me a thousand times thou never shouldst love woman like me.

VIOLA   And all those sayings will I over-swear!

DUKE   Give me thy hand. You shall from this time be your master's mistress!

OLIVIA   (*gazing from Sebastian to Viola*) A sister! You are she!

In the midst of all the embracings and smiles comes Malvolio, unkempt, with straw in his hair and rage in his eyes. Feste follows.

MALVOLIO   Madam, you have done me wrong, notorious wrong!

OLIVIA   Have I, Malvolio? No.

MALVOLIO　Lady, you have. Pray you, peruse that letter. (*Gives her the fatal letter*.) You must not now deny it is your hand. Tell me, in the modesty of honour, why you have given me such clear lights of favour, bade me come smiling and cross-gartered to you? Why have you suffered me to be imprisoned, kept in a dark house? Tell me, why?

OLIVIA　Alas, Malvolio, this is not my writing—

FESTE　Good madam, hear me speak. Most freely I confess, myself and Toby set this device against Malvolio here. Maria writ the letter, at Sir Toby's great importance, in recompense whereof he hath married her—

OLIVIA　Alas, poor fool, how have they baffled thee.

MALVOLIO　I'll be revenged on the whole pack of you!

He stalks away in high indignation.

OLIVIA　He hath been most notoriously abused.

DUKE　Pursue him, and entreat him to a peace. Cesario, come; for so you shall be while you are a man; but when in other habits you are seen, Orsino's mistress and his fancy's queen.

The lovers, in pairs, go within the mansion gates. Only Feste is left behind. He seats himself outside the gate and sings:

FESTE

When that I was and a little tiny boy,
With hey, ho, the wind and the rain,
A foolish thing was but a toy,
For the rain it raineth every day.
But when I came to man's estate,
With hey, ho, the wind and the rain,
'Gainst knaves and thieves men shut their gate,
For the rain it raineth every day.
A great while ago the world begun,
With hey, ho, the wind and the rain,
But that's all one, our play is done,
And we'll strive to please you every day.

The curtain falls . . .